Plant Based Diet Cookbook for Beginners

A Beginner's Guide on How to Use Plant Based Diet to Burn Fat Rapidly

Rebecca Queen

By reading this document, the reader agrees that under no circumstances is the author responsible for any losses, direct or indirect, which are incurred as a result of the use of information contained within this document, including, but not limited to, errors, omissions, or inaccuracies.

Table of Content

BREAKFAST 9

.... 9

SWEET POTATO SLICES WITH FRUITS..10
BREAKFAST OAT BROWNIES 12
AMARANTH QUINOA PORRIDGE 14
CHOC-BANANA SMOOTHIE 16
CACAO LENTIL MUFFINS 17
SPINACH TOFU SCRAMBLE WITH SOUR CREAM 19
PEANUT BUTTER BANANA QUINOA BOWL 21
ORANGE PUMPKIN PANCAKES 23
MEXICAN BREAKFAST 25
BERRY BLAST SMOOTHIE..27
GREENS AND BERRY SMOOTHIE 28
OVERNIGHT CHIA OATS..29

MAINS... 31

....31

TEMPEH SKEWERS WITH DRESSING...32
CHILI QUINOA STUFFED PEPPERS 35
RED BURGERS 37
HEMP FALAFEL WITH TAHINI SAUCE 39
STUFFED SWEET HUMMUS POTATOES 41
SPICY BEANS AND RICE 43
CRUSTED TOFU STEAKS WITH CARAMELIZED ONION 45
LENTILS BOLOGNESE WITH SOBA NOODLES 48
WHITE BEAN SALAD WITH SPICY SAUCE 50

SIDES AND SALADS 52

.... 52

SESAME SEED SIMPLE MIX..53
NIÇOISE SALAD 54
AVOCADO KALE SALAD 56
VEGETABLE SALAD WITH CHIMICHURRI 58
CHERRY TOMATO SALAD WITH SOY CHORIZO...............................61
ROASTED SQUASH SALAD 62

THAI SALAD WITH TEMPEH 64

SOUPS AND STEWS 67

....67

SWEET POTATO SOUP... 68
PEARL BARLEY TOMATO MUSHROOM SOUP 69
GREEK LENTIL SOUP.. 70
ZUCCHINI-DILL BOWLS WITH RICOTTA CHEESE........................ 72
CORN CHOWDER 73
ITALIAN PLUM TOMATO SOUP 75
ARTICHOKE BEAN SOUP... 77
BROCCOLI WHITE BEAN SOUP.. 79
CHINESE RICE SOUP 81
BALSAMIC HATCHET SOUP 83
CAULIFLOWER SOUP 85
AFRICAN LENTIL SOUP... 87

SNACK 89

BEETROOT HUMMUS... 89
SEASONED POTATOES 91
SPINACH STUFFED PORTOBELLO 93
MUSHROOM STUFFED TOMATOES... 94
BLACK BEAN LIME DIP 97

SAUCES, AND CONDIMENTS 99

HOT SAUCE 99
SPICY RED WINE TOMATO SAUCE 100
HOT SAUCE 102
VODKA CREAM SAUCE.. 103

DESSERTS AND DRINKS 105

....105

LEMON SQUARES 106
GREEN POPSICLE 108
TANGERINE CAKE... 110
FUDGE POPSICLES.. 110
GRAPE PUDDING 113
STRAWBERRY COCONUT POPSICLES 115
SWEET CASHEW STICKS 117
SWEET TOMATO BREAD 118

BREAKFAST

Sweet Potato Slices With Fruits

Preparation time: 10 minutes

Cooking time: 10 minutes

Servings: 2

Ingredients:

The base:

- 1 sweet potato

Topping:

- 60g organic peanut butter
- 30ml pure maple syrup
- 4 dried apricots, sliced
- 30g fresh raspberries

Directions:

1. Peel and cut sweet potato into ½ cm thick slices.
2. Place the potato slices in a toaster on high for 5 minutes. Toast your sweet potatoes TWICE.
3. Arrange sweet potato slices onto a plate.
4. Spread the peanut butter over sweet potato slices.
5. Drizzle the maple syrup over the butter.
6. Top each slice with an equal amount of sliced apricots and raspberries.
7. Serve.

Nutrition:

Calories 300

Total Fat 16.9g

Total Carbohydrate 32.1g

Dietary Fiber 6.2g

Total Sugars 17.7g

Protein 10.3g

Breakfast Oat Brownies

Preparation time: 10 minutes

Cooking time: 40 minutes

Servings: 10 slices (2 per serving

Ingredients:

- 180g old-fashioned rolled oats
- 80g peanut flour
- 30g chickpea flour
- 25g flax seeds meal
- 5g baking powder, aluminum-free
- ½ teaspoon baking soda
- 5ml vanilla paste
- 460ml unsweetened vanilla soy milk
- 80g organic applesauce
- 55g organic pumpkin puree
- 45g organic peanut butter
- 5ml liquid stevia extract
- 25g slivered almonds

Directions:

1. Preheat oven to 180C/350F.
2. Line 18cm baking pan with parchment paper, leaving overhanging sides.

3. In a large bowl, combine oats, peanut flour, chickpea flour, flax seeds, baking powder, and baking soda.
4. In a separate bowl, whisk together vanilla paste, soy milk, applesauce. Pumpkin puree, peanut butter, and stevia.
5. Fold the liquid ingredients into dry ones and stir until incorporated.
6. Pour the batter into the prepared baking pan.
7. Sprinkle evenly with slivered almonds.
8. Bake the oat brownies for 40 minutes.
9. Remove from the oven and place aside to cool.
10. Slice and serve.

Nutrition:

Calories 309

Total Fat 15.3g

Total Carbohydrate 32.2g

Dietary Fiber 9.2g

Total Sugars 9.1g

Protein 13.7g

Amaranth Quinoa Porridge

Preparation time: 5 minutes

Cooking time: 35 minutes

Servings: 2

Ingredients:

- 85g quinoa
- 70g amaranth
- 460ml water
- 115ml unsweetened soy milk
- ½ teaspoon vanilla paste
- 15g almond butter
- 30ml pure maple syrup
- 10g raw pumpkin seeds
- 10g pomegranate seeds

Directions:

1. Combine quinoa, amaranth, and water.
2. Bring to a boil over medium-high heat.
3. Reduce heat and simmer the grains, stirring occasionally, for 20 minutes.
4. Stir in milk and maple syrup.
5. Simmer for 6-7 minutes. Remove from the heat and stir in vanilla, and almond butter.
6. Allow the mixture to stand for 5 minutes.
7. Divide the porridge between two bowls.

8. Top with pumpkin seeds and pomegranate seeds.

9. Serve.

Nutrition:

Calories 474

Total Fat 13.3g

Total Carbohydrate 73.2g

Dietary Fiber 8.9g

Total Sugars 10g

Protein 17.8g

Choc-Banana Smoothie

Preparation time: 3 minutes

Servings: 2

Ingredients

- 1 banana
- 2 tbsp. hemp seeds
- 2/3 cup water
- 2 cups ice
- 1 cup almond or cashew milk
- 2 scoop Vegan chocolate protein powder
- 2 tbsp. cacao powder

Directions:

1. Pop everything in a blender and blitz
2. Pour into glasses and serve.

Nutrition:

Calories 676, Total Fat 52.3g, Saturated Fat 38.1g, Cholesterol 0mg, Sodium 46mg, Total Carbohydrate 41.6g, Dietary Fiber 8.7g, Total Sugars 25.2g, Protein 22.4g, Vitamin D 0mcg, Calcium 80mg, Iron 6mg, Potassium 528mg

Cacao Lentil Muffins

Preparation time: 10 minutes

Cooking time: 15 minutes

Servings: 12 muffins (2 per serving

Ingredients:

- 195g cooked red lentils
- 50ml melted coconut oil
- 45ml pure maple syrup
- 60ml unsweetened almond milk
- 60ml water
- 60g raw cocoa powder
- 120g whole-wheat flour
- 20g peanut flour
- 10g baking powder, aluminum-free
- 70g Vegan chocolate chips

Directions:

1. Preheat oven to 200C/400F.
2. Line 12-hole muffin tin with paper cases.
3. Place the cooked red lentils in a food blender. Blend on high until smooth.
4. Transfer the lentils puree into a large bowl.
5. Stir in coconut oil, maple syrup, almond milk, and water.
6. In a separate bowl, whisk cocoa powder, whole-wheat

flour, peanut flour, and baking powder.

7. Fold in liquid ingredients and stir until just combined.

8. Add chocolate chips and stir until incorporated.

9. Divide the batter among 12 paper cases.

10. Tap the muffin tin gently onto the kitchen counter to remove air.

11. Bake the muffins for 15 minutes.

12. Cool muffins on a wire rack.

13. Serve.

Nutrition:

Calories 372

Total Fat 13.5g

Total Carbohydrate 52.7g

Dietary Fiber 12.9g

Total Sugars 13g

Protein 13.7g

Spinach Tofu Scramble With Sour Cream

Preparation time: 10 minutes

Cooking time: 15 minutes

Servings: 2

Ingredients:

Sour cream:

- 75g raw cashews, soaked overnight
- 30ml lemon juice
- 5g nutritional yeast
- 60ml water
- 1 good pinch salt

Tofu scramble:

- 15ml olive oil
- 1 small onion, diced
- 1 clove garlic, minced
- 400 firm tofu, pressed, crumbled
- ½ teaspoon ground cumin
- ½ teaspoon curry powder
- ½ teaspoon turmeric
- 2 tomatoes, diced
- 30g baby spinach
- Salt, to taste

Directions:

1. Make the cashew sour cream; rinse and drain soaked

cashews.

2. Place the cashews, lemon juice, nutritional yeast, water, and salt in a food processor.

3. Blend on high until smooth, for 5-6 minutes.

4. Transfer to a bowl and place aside.

5. Make the tofu scramble; heat olive oil in a skillet.

6. Add onion and Cooking Time: 5 minutes over medium-high.

7. Add garlic, and Cooking Time: stirring, for 1 minute.

8. Add crumbled tofu, and stir to coat with oil.

9. Add the cumin, curry, and turmeric. Cooking Time: the tofu for 2 minutes.

10. Add the tomatoes and Cooking Time: for 2 minutes.

11. Add spinach and cook, tossing until completely wilted, about 1 minute.

12. Transfer tofu scramble on the plate.

13. Top with a sour cream and serve.

Nutrition:

Calories 411

Total Fat 26.5g

Total Carbohydrate 23.1g

Dietary Fiber 5.9g

Total Sugars 6.3g

Protein 25g

Peanut Butter Banana Quinoa Bowl

Preparation time: 15 minutes

Cooking time: 15 minutes

Servings: 1

Ingredients:

- 175ml unsweetened soy milk
- 85g uncooked quinoa
- ½ teaspoon Ceylon cinnamon
- 10g chia seeds
- 30g organic peanut butter
- 30ml unsweetened almond milk
- 10g raw cocoa powder
- 5 drops liquid stevia
- 1 small banana, peeled, sliced

Directions:

1. In a saucepan, bring soy milk, quinoa, and Ceylon cinnamon to a boil.
2. Reduce heat and simmer 15 minutes.
3. Remove from the heat and stir in Chia seeds. Cover the saucepan with lid and place aside for 15 minutes.
4. In the meantime, microwave peanut butter and almond milk for 30 seconds on high. Remove and stir until runny. Repeat the process if needed.
5. Stir in raw cocoa powder and Stevia.
6. To serve; fluff the quinoa with fork and transfer in a

bowl.

7. Top with sliced banana.

8. Drizzle the quinoa with peanut butter.

9. Serve.

Nutrition:

Calories 718

Total Fat 29.6g

Total Carbohydrate 90.3g

Dietary Fiber 17.5g

Total Sugars 14.5g

Protein 30.4g

Orange Pumpkin Pancakes

Preparation time: 10 minutes

Cooking time: 15 minutes

Servings: 4

Ingredients:

- 10g ground flax meal
- 45ml water
- 235ml unsweetened soy milk
- 15ml lemon juice
- 60g buckwheat flour
- 60g all-purpose flour
- 8g baking powder, aluminum-free
- 2 teaspoons finely grated orange zest
- 25g white chia seeds
- 120g organic pumpkin puree (or just bake the pumpkin and puree the flesh
- 30ml melted and cooled coconut oil
- 5ml vanilla paste
- 30ml pure maple syrup

Directions:

1. Combine ground flax meal with water in a small bowl. Place aside for 10 minutes.
2. Combine almond milk and cider vinegar in a medium bowl. Place aside for 5 minutes.

3. In a separate large bowl, combine buckwheat flour, all-purpose flour, baking powder, orange zest, and chia seeds.
4. Pour in almond milk, along with pumpkin puree, coconut oil, vanilla, and maple syrup.
5. Whisk together until you have a smooth batter.
6. Heat large non-stick skillet over medium-high heat. Brush the skillet gently with some coconut oil.
7. Pour 60ml of batter into skillet. Cooking Time: the pancake for 1 minute, or until bubbles appear on the surface.
8. Lift the pancake gently with a spatula and flip.
9. Cooking Time: 1 ½ minutes more. Slide the pancake onto a plate. Repeat with the remaining batter.
10. Serve warm.

Nutrition:

Calories 301

Total Fat 12.6g

Total Carbohydrate 41.7g

Dietary Fiber 7.2g

Total Sugars 9.9g

Protein 8.1g

Mexican Breakfast

Preparation time: 10 minutes

Cooking time: 10 minutes

Servings: 4

Ingredients:

- 170g cherry tomatoes, halved
- 1 small red onion, chopped
- 25ml lime juice
- 50ml olive oil
- 1 clove garlic, minced
- 1 teaspoon red chili flakes
- 1 teaspoon ground cumin
- 700g can black beans* (or cooked beans), rinsed
- 4 slices whole-grain bread
- 1 avocado, peeled, pitted
- Salt, to taste

Directions:

1. Combine tomatoes, onion, lime juice, and 15ml olive oil in a bowl.
2. Season to taste and place aside.
3. Heat 2 tablespoons olive oil in a skillet.
4. Add onion and Cooking Time: 4 minutes over medium-high heat.
5. Add garlic and Cooking Time: stirring for 1 minute.

6. Add red chili flakes and cumin. Cooking Time: for 30 seconds.

7. Add beans and Cooking Time: tossing gently for 2 minutes.

8. Stir in ¾ of the tomato mixture and season to taste.

9. Remove from heat.

10. Slice the avocado very thinly.

11. Spread the beans mixture over bread slices. Top with remaining tomato and sliced avocado.

12. Serve.

Nutrition:

Calories 476

Total Fat 21.9g

Total Carbohydrate 52.4g

Dietary Fiber 19.5g

Total Sugars 5.3g

Protein 17.1g

Berry Blast Smoothie

Preparation time: 3 minutes

Servings: 2

Ingredients

- 1 cup raspberries
- 1 cup frozen blueberries
- 1 cup frozen blackberries
- 1 cup almond milk
- ¼ cup Soy Yogurt

Directions:

1. Pop everything in a blender and blitz
2. Pour into glasses and serve.

Nutrition:

Calories 404, Total Fat 30.4g, Saturated Fat 25.5g, Cholesterol 0mg, Sodium 22mg, Total Carbohydrate 34.5g, Dietary Fiber 12.5g, Total Sugars 19.6g, Protein 6.3g, Vitamin D 0mcg, Calcium 112mg, Iron 4mg, Potassium 581mg

Greens and Berry Smoothie

Preparation time: 3 minutes

Servings 2

Ingredients

- 1 cup frozen berries
- 1 cup kale or spinach
- ¾ cup milk almond, oat or coconut milk
- ½ tbsp chia seeds

Directions:

1. Pop everything in a blender and blitz
2. Pour into glasses and serve.

Nutrition:

Calories 298, Saturated Fat 19.3g, Cholesterol 0mg, Sodium 29mg, Total Carbohydrate 20g, Dietary Fiber 7.4g, Total Sugars 8g, Protein 4.7g, Vitamin D 0mcg, Calcium 114mg, Iron 3mg, Potassium 520mg

Overnight Chia Oats

Preparation time: 15minutes + inactive time

Cooking time: 20 minutes

Servings: 4

Ingredients:

- 470ml full-fat soy milk
- 90g old-fashioned rolled oats
- 40g chia seeds
- 15ml pure maple syrup
- 25g crushed pistachios
- Blackberry Jam:
- 500g blackberries
- 45ml pure maple syrup
- 30ml water
- 45g chia seeds
- 15ml lemon juice

Directions:

1. Make the oats; in a large bowl, combine soy milk, oats, chia seeds, and maple syrup.
2. Cover and refrigerate overnight.
3. Make the jam; combine blackberries, maple syrup, and water in a saucepan.
4. Simmer over medium heat for 10 minutes.
5. Add the chia seeds and simmer the blackberries for 10

minutes.

6. Remove from heat and stir in lemon juice. Mash the blackberries with a fork and place aside to cool.

7. Assemble; divide the oatmeal among four serving bowls.

8. Top with each bowl blackberry jam.

9. Sprinkle with pistachios before serving.

Nutrition:

Calories 362

Total Fat 13.4g

Total Carbohydrate 52.6g

Dietary Fiber 17.4g

Total Sugars 24.6g

Protein 12.4g

MAINS

Tempeh Skewers With Dressing

Preparation time: 20 minutes

Cooking time: 10 minutes

Servings: 6

Ingredients:

- 445g tempeh, cut into fingers
- 155ml unsweetened almond milk
- 100g almond flour
- 8g paprika
- 4g garlic powder
- 3g dried basil
- Salt and pepper, to taste
- 15ml olive oil

Finger sauce:

- 60ml melted coconut oil
- 80g hot sauce
- 10 drops Stevia

Dressing:

- 230g vegan mayonnaise
- 115g vegan sour cream
- 1 clove garlic, minced
- 2g chopped dill
- 2g chopped chives
- 1g onion powder

- Salt and pepper, to taste

Directions:

1. Cut the tempeh into slices/fingers. Arrange onto bamboo skewers, soaked in water 30 minutes.
2. Bring a pot of water to a boil. Add tempeh and boil 15 minutes. Drain and place aside.
3. Heat oven to 200C/400F.
4. Pour almond milk into a bowl. Combine almond flour and spices into a separate bowl.
5. Dip the tempeh into almond milk, and coat with the almond flour mixture.
6. Grease baking sheet with coconut oil. Arrange the tempeh fingers onto a baking sheet.
7. Bake the tempeh 10 minutes. In the meantime, make the sauce.
8. Melt coconut oil in a saucepan. Add hot sauce and simmer 5minutes. Add Stevia and remove from the heat.
9. Make the dressing by combining all ingredients together.
10. Toss the tempeh with hot sauce. Serve with prepared dressing.

Nutrition:

Calories 351

Total Fat 29.3g

Total Carbohydrate 9.9g

Dietary Fiber 1g

Total Sugars 0.2g

Protein 15.5g

Chili Quinoa Stuffed Peppers

Preparation time: 15 minutes

Cooking time: 1 hour 5 minutes

Servings: 4

Ingredients:

- 160g quinoa
- 460ml vegetable stock
- 2 red bell peppers, cut in half, seeds and membrane removed
- 2 yellow bell peppers, cut in half, seeds, and membrane removed
- 120g salsa
- 15g nutritional yeast
- 10g chili powder
- 5g cumin powder
- 425g can black beans, rinsed, drained
- 160g fresh corn kernels
- Salt and pepper, to taste
- 1 small avocado, sliced
- 15g chopped cilantro

Directions:

1. Preheat oven to 190C/375F.
2. Brush the baking sheet with some cooking oil.
3. Combine quinoa and vegetable stock in a saucepan.

Bring to a boil.

4. Reduce heat and simmer 20 minutes.
5. Transfer the quinoa to a large bowl.
6. Stir in salsa, nutritional yeast, chili powder, cumin powder, black beans, and corn. Season to taste with salt and pepper.
7. Stuff the bell pepper halves with prepared mixture.
8. Transfer the peppers onto a baking sheet, cover with aluminum foil, and bake for 30 minutes.
9. Increase heat to 200C/400F and bake the peppers for an additional 15 minutes.
10. Serve warm, topped with avocado slices, and chopped cilantro.

Nutrition:

Calories 456

Total Fat 15.4g

Total Carbohydrate 71.1g

Dietary Fiber 15.8g

Total Sugars 8.2g

Protein 17.4g

Red Burgers

Preparation time: 10 minutes

Cooking time: 50 minutes

Servings: 4

Ingredients:

Patties:

- 2 large beets, peeled, cubed
- 1 red onion, cut into chunks
- 115g red kidney beans
- 85g red cooked quinoa
- 2 cloves garlic, minced
- 30g almond meal
- 20g ground flax
- 10ml lemon juice
- ½ teaspoon ground cumin
- ½ teaspoon red pepper flakes
- Salt, to taste
- 4 whole-meal burger buns

Tahini Guacamole:

- 1 avocado, pitted, peeled
- 45ml lime juice
- 30g tahini sauce
- 5g chopped coriander

Directions:

1. Preheat oven to 190C/375F.
2. Toss beet and onion with a splash of olive oil.
3. Season with salt. Bake the beets for 30 minutes.
4. Transfer the beets and onion into a food blender.
5. Add the beans and blend until coarse. You do not want a completely smooth mixture.
6. Stir in quinoa, garlic, almond meal, flax seeds, lemon juice, cumin, and red pepper flakes.
7. Shape the mixture into four patties.
8. Transfer the patties to a baking sheet, lined with parchment paper.
9. Bake the patties 20 minutes, flipping halfway through.
10. In the meantime, make the tahini guac; mash the avocado with lime juice in a bowl.
11. Stir in tahini and coriander. Season to taste.
12. To serve; place the patty in the bun, top with guacamole and serve.

Nutrition:

Calories 343

Total Fat 16.6g

Total Carbohydrate 49.1g

Dietary Fiber 14.4g

Total Sugars 8.1g

Protein 15g

Hemp Falafel With Tahini Sauce

Preparation time: 10 minutes

Cooking time: 10 minutes

Servings: 6

Ingredients:

- 80g raw hemp hearts
- 4g chopped cilantro
- 4g chopped basil
- 2 cloves garlic, minced
- 2g ground cumin seeds
- 3g chili powder
- 14g flax meal + 30ml filtered water
- Sea salt and pepper, to taste
- Avocado or coconut oil, to fry

Sauce:

- 115g tahini
- 60ml fresh lime juice
- 115ml filtered water
- 30ml extra-virgin olive oil
- Sea salt, to taste
- A good pinch ground cumin seeds

Directions:

1. Mix flax with filtered water in a small bowl.
2. Place aside for 10 minutes.

3. In meantime, combine raw hemp hearts, cilantro, basil, garlic, cumin, chili, and seasonings in a food processor.

4. Process until just comes together. Add the flax seeds mixture and process until finely blended and uniform.

5. Heat approximately 2 tablespoons avocado oil in a skillet. Shape 1 tablespoon mixture into balls and fry for 3-4 minutes or until deep golden brown.

6. Remove from the skillet and place on a plate lined with paper towels.

7. Make the sauce; combine all ingredients in a food blender. Blend until smooth and creamy.

8. Serve falafel with fresh lettuce salad and tahini sauce.

Nutrition:

Calories 347

Total Fat 29.9g

Total Carbohydrate 7.2g

Dietary Fiber 4.3g

Total Sugars 0.2g

Protein 13.8g

Stuffed Sweet Hummus Potatoes

Preparation time: 10 minutes

Cooking time: 15 minutes

Servings: 4

Ingredients:

- 4 large sweet potatoes
- 10ml olive oil
- 200g kale, stems removed, chopped
- 300g can black beans, drained, rinsed
- 240g hummus
- 60ml water
- 5g garlic powder
- Salt and pepper, to taste
- Sour cream:
- 100g raw cashews, soaked in water for 4 hours
- 80ml water
- 15ml raw cider vinegar
- 15ml lemon juice
- 1 pinch salt

Directions:

1. Prick sweet potato with a fork or toothpick all over the surface.
2. Wrap the potato in a damp paper towel and place in a microwave.

3. Microwave the sweet potato 10 minutes or until fork tender.
4. In the meantime, heat olive oil in a skillet.
5. Add kale and Cooking Time: with a pinch of salt until wilted.
6. Add black beans and Cooking Time: 2 minutes.
7. Make the sour cream; combine all sour cream ingredients in a food processor.
8. Process until creamy. Chill briefly before serving.
9. Make a slit in each sweet potato.
10. Combine hummus, water, and garlic powder in a bowl.
11. Stuff potato with the kale-bean mixture. Top the sweet potato with hummus and a dollop of sour cream.
12. Serve.

Nutrition:

Calories 540

Total Fat 20.3g2

Total Carbohydrate 78.1g

Dietary Fiber 14.9g

Total Sugars 3g

Protein 16.6g

Spicy Beans And Rice

Preparation time: 10 minutes

Cooking time: 1 hour 10 minutes

Servings: 6

Ingredients:

- 450g dry red kidney beans, soaked overnight
- 15ml olive oil
- 1 onion, diced
- 1 red bell pepper, seeded, diced
- 1 large stalk celery, sliced
- 4 cloves garlic, minced
- 15ml hot sauce
- 5g paprika
- 2g dried thyme
- 2 g parsley, chopped
- 2 bay leaves
- 900ml vegetable stock
- 280g brown rice
- Salt and pepper, to taste

Directions:

1. Drain the beans and place aside.
2. Heat olive oil in a saucepot.
3. Add onion and bell pepper. Cooking Time: 6 minutes.
4. Add celery and Cooking Time: 3 minutes.

5. Add garlic, hot sauce, paprika, and thyme. Cooking Time: 1 minute.

6. Add the drained beans, bay leaves, and vegetable stock.

7. Bring to a boil, and reduce heat.

8. Simmer the beans for 1 hour 15 minutes or until tender.

9. In the meantime, place rice in a small saucepot. Cover the rice with 4cm water.

10. Season to taste and Cooking Time: the rice until tender, for 25 minutes.

11. To serve; transfer ¼ of the beans into a food processor. Process until smooth.

12. Combine the processed beans with the remaining beans and ladle into a bowl.

13. Add rice and sprinkle with parsley before serving.

Nutrition:

Calories 469

Total Fat 6g

Total Carbohydrate 87.5g

Dietary Fiber 14.2g

Total Sugars 4.9g

Protein 21.1g

Crusted Tofu Steaks With Caramelized Onion

Preparation time: 15 minutes

Cooking time: 45 minutes

Servings: 4

Ingredients:

- 450g tofu, cut into 8 steaks/slices
- 100g graham crackers
- 80g raw cashews
- 230ml unsweetened soy milk
- 120g whole-wheat flour
- 10g garlic powder
- 10g onion powder
- 10g chili powder
- 5g lemon pepper
- 15ml olive oil
- Salt, to taste

Onion:

- 15ml grapeseed oil
- 1 large onion
- 15ml balsamic vinegar
- 15ml lemon juice
- 15ml water
- 15g maple sugar

Directions:

1. Make the tofu; preheat oven to 200C/400F and line a baking sheet with parchment paper.
2. Combine graham crackers and cashews in a food processor.
3. Process unto coarse crumbs form.
4. Transfer to a large bowl.
5. In a separate bowl, combine flour, garlic and onion powder, chili, and lemon pepper.
6. Pour the soy milk into a third bowl.
7. Coat tofu with flour, dip into milk and finally coat with the graham cracker crumbs.
8. Arrange the tofu steaks onto a baking sheet.
9. Bake the tofu for 15-20 minutes or until golden brown.
10. In the meantime, make the onion; heat grapeseed oil in a skillet.
11. Add onion and Cooking Time: over medium-high heat for 8 minutes.
12. Add balsamic, lemon juice, and maple sugar. Cooking Time: 2 minutes.
13. Add water and reduce heat. Simmer 15 minutes.
14. Serve tofu steaks with caramelized onions.

Nutrition:

Calories 617

Total Fat 29.5g

Total Carbohydrate 70.6g

Dietary Fiber 5.8g

Total Sugars 17g

Protein 23.6g

Lentils Bolognese With Soba Noodles

Preparation time: 10 minutes

Cooking time: 15 minutes (plus 25 for lentils

Servings: 4

Ingredients:

Bolognese:

- 100g red lentils
- 1 bay leaf
- Splash of olive oil
- 1 small onion, diced
- 1 large stalk celery, sliced
- 3 cloves garlic, minced
- 230ml tomato sauce or fresh pureed tomatoes
- 60ml red wine or vegetable stock (if you do not like wine
- 1 tablespoon fresh basil, chopped
- Salt and pepper, to taste

Soba noodles:

- 280g soba noodles

Directions:

1. Cooking Time: the lentils; place lentils and bay leaf in a saucepan.
2. Cover with water, so the water is 2-inches above the lentils.

3. Bring to a boil over medium-high heat.

4. Reduce heat and simmer the lentils for 25 minutes.

5. Drain the lentils and discard the bay leaf.

6. Heat a splash of olive oil in a saucepan.

7. Add onion, and Cooking Time: 6 minutes.

8. Add celery and Cooking Time: 2 minutes.

9. Add garlic and Cooking Time: 2 minutes.

10. Add the tomatoes and wine. Simmer the mixture for 5 minutes.

11. Stir in the lentils and simmer 2 minutes.

12. Remove the Bolognese from the heat and stir in basil.

13. In the meantime, Cooking Time: the soba noodles according to package directions.

14. Serve noodles with lentils Bolognese.

Nutrition:

Calories 353

Total Fat 0.9g

Total Carbohydrate 74g

Dietary Fiber 9g

Total Sugars 4.2g

Protein 17.7g

White Bean Salad With Spicy Sauce

Preparation time: 15 minutes

Servings: 4

Ingredients:

- 450g can white beans, rinsed, drained or cooked beans
- 1 avocado, peeled, chopped
- 6 cherry tomatoes, quartered
- 1 red onion, thinly sliced

Sauce:

- 80g cashews, soaked in water 4 hours
- 30ml extra-virgin olive oil
- 30ml lemon juice
- 70ml water
- 10g Dijon mustard
- 5g pure maple syrup
- 1 clove garlic
- ½ teaspoon cayenne pepper
- ½ teaspoon paprika powder
- 1 pinch salt

Directions:

1. Make the sauce; rinse and drain cashews and place in a food processor.
2. Add the remaining ingredients, olive oil, lemon juice, water, mustard, garlic, cayenne, paprika, and salt.

3. Process until smooth and creamy. Place aside.
4. Make the salad; prepared vegetables as described.
5. Toss the beans with avocado, cherry tomatoes, and red onion.
6. Drizzle with prepared dressing and toss once again.
7. Serve or refrigerate before serving.

Nutrition:

Calories 366

Total Fat 24.2g

Total Carbohydrate 31.9g

Dietary Fiber 9.5g

Total Sugars 5.6g

Protein 11g

SIDES AND SALADS

Sesame Seed Simple Mix

Preparation Time: 5minutes

Servings: 2

Ingredients

- Frozen peas: 1 cup can washed and drained
- Corn kernel: 2 cups can
- Salt: as per your taste
- Sesame seeds: 2 tbsp
- Pepper: as per your taste
- Cashew cream: ½ cup

Directions:

1. Combine all the ingredients
2. Serve as the side dish

Nutrition:

Carbs: 44.5g

Protein: 11.5g

Fats: 11.4g

Calories: 306Kcal

Niçoise Salad

Preparation time: 10 minutes

Cooking time: 15 minutes

Total time: 25 minutes

Servings: 04

Ingredients:

Salad:

- 6 small red potatoes, peeled, boiled, and diced
- 1 cup green beans, chopped
- 1 head lettuce, chopped
- ½ cup pitted kalamata olives
- ½ cup tomato, sliced
- ½medium red beet

Chickpeas:

- 1 (15 ouncecan chickpeas
- 1 teaspoon Dijon mustard
- 1 teaspoon maple syrup
- 1 teaspoon dried dill
- 1 pinch salt
- 1 tablespoon roasted sunflower seeds

Dressing:

- 3 tablespoons minced shallot
- 1 heaping teaspoon Dijon mustard
- 1 teaspoon fresh thyme, chopped

- ⅓ cup red wine vinegar
- ¼ teaspoon salt and black pepper
- ¼ cup olive oil

How to Prepare:

1. Preheat your oven to 400 degrees F.
2. In a greased baking sheet, toss chickpeas with salt and all the chickpea ingredients.
3. Bake the chickpeas for 15 minutes in the oven.
4. Combine all the dressing ingredients in a small bowl.
5. In a salad bowl, toss in all the vegetables, roasted chickpeas, and dressing.
6. Mix them well then refrigerate to chill.
7. Serve.

Nutritional Values:

Calories 205

Total Fat 22.7 g

Saturated Fat 6.1 g

Cholesterol 4 mg

Sodium 227 mg

Total Carbs 26.1 g

Fiber 1.4 g

Sugar 0.9 g

Protein 5.2 g

Avocado Kale Salad

Preparation time: 10 minutes

Cooking time: 0 minutes

Total time: 10 minutes

Servings: 04

Ingredients:

Dressing:

- ⅓ cup tahini
- 2 teaspoons garlic, chopped
- 1 medium lemon juiced
- 1½ tablespoons maple syrup
- Water

Salad:

- 1 large bundle kale, chopped
- 1 tablespoon grapeseed oil
- 1 tablespoon lemon juice
- 1 medium beet

How to Prepare:

1. Combine all the dressing ingredients in a small bowl.
2. In a salad bowl, toss in all the salad ingredients and dressing.
3. Mix them well then refrigerate to chill.
4. Serve.

Nutritional Values:

Calories 201

Total Fat 8.9 g

Saturated Fat 4.5 g

Cholesterol 57 mg

Sodium 340 mg

Total Carbs 24.7 g

Fiber 1.2 g

Sugar 1.3 g

Protein 15.3 g

Vegetable Salad With Chimichurri

Preparation time: 10 minutes

Cooking time: 25 minutes

Total time: 35 minutes

Servings: 04

Ingredients:

Roasted vegetables:

- 1 large sweet potato (chopped
- 6 red potatoes, quartered
- 2 whole carrots, chopped
- 2 tablespoons melted coconut oil
- 2 teaspoons curry powder
- ½ teaspoon salt
- 1 cup chopped broccolini
- 2 cups red cabbage, chopped
- 1 medium red bell pepper, sliced

Chimichurri:

- 5 cloves garlic, chopped
- 1 medium serrano pepper
- 1 cup packed cilantro
- 1 cup parsley
- 3 tablespoons ripe avocado
- ¼ teaspoon salt
- 3 tablespoons lime juice

- 1 tablespoon maple syrup
- Water to thin

Salad:

- 4 cups hearty greens
- 1 medium ripe avocado, chopped
- 3 tablespoons hemp seeds
- Fresh herbs
- 5 medium radishes, sliced
- ¼ cup macadamia nut cheese

How to Prepare:

1. Preheat your oven to 400 degrees F.
2. In a suitable bowl, toss all the vegetables for roasting with salt, curry powder and oil.
3. Divide these vegetables into two roasting pans.
4. Bake the vegetables for 25 minutes in the oven.
5. Meanwhile, in a blender, blend all chimichurri sauce ingredients until smooth.
6. In a salad bowl, toss in all the roasted vegetables, chimichurri sauce and salad ingredients.
7. Mix them well then refrigerate to chill.
8. Serve.

Nutritional Values:

Calories 231

Total Fat 20.1 g

Saturated Fat 2.4 g

Cholesterol 110 mg

Sodium 941 mg

Total Carbs 20.1 g

Fiber 0.9 g

Sugar 1.4 g

Protein 4.6 g

Cherry Tomato Salad With Soy Chorizo

Preparation Time: 5 minutes

Cooking Time: 5 minutes

Serving Size: 4

Ingredients:

- 2 ½ tbsp olive oil
- 4 soy chorizo, chopped
- 2 tsp red wine vinegar
- 1 small red onion, finely chopped
- 2 ½ cups cherry tomatoes, halved
- 2 tbsp chopped cilantro
- Salt and freshly ground black pepper to taste
- 3 tbsp sliced black olives to garnish

Directions:

1. Over medium fire, heat half tablespoon of olive oil in a skillet and fry soy chorizo until golden. Turn heat off.
2. In a salad bowl, whisk remaining olive oil and vinegar. Add onion, cilantro, tomatoes, and soy chorizo. Mix with dressing and season with salt and black pepper.
3. Garnish with olives and serve.

Nutrition:

Calories 138, Total Fat 8.95g, Total Carbs 5.63g, Fiber 0.4g, Net Carbs 5.23g, Protein 7.12g

Roasted Squash Salad

Preparation time: 10 minutes

Cooking time: 20 minutes

Total time: 30 minutes

Servings: 04

Ingredients:

Squash:

- 1 medium acorn squash, peeled and cubed
- 1 tablespoon avocado oil
- 1 pinch each salt and black pepper

Dressing:

- 1 cup balsamic vinegar

Salad:

- ¼ cup macadamia nut cheese
- 2 tablespoons roasted pumpkin seeds
- 5 cups arugula
- 2 tablespoons dried currants

How to Prepare:

1. Preheat your oven to 425 degrees F.
2. On a greased baking sheet, toss squash with salt, black pepper, and oil.
3. Bake the seasoned squash for 20 minutes in the oven.
4. Combine all the dressing ingredients in a small bowl.
5. In a salad bowl, toss in the squash, salad ingredients,

and dressing.

6. Mix them well then refrigerate to chill.

7. Serve.

Nutritional Values:

Calories 119

Total Fat 14 g

Saturated Fat 2 g

Cholesterol 65 mg

Sodium 269 mg

Total Carbs 19 g

Fiber 4 g

Sugar 6 g

Protein 5g

Thai Salad With Tempeh

Preparation time: 10 minutes

Cooking time: 0 minutes

Total time: 10 minutes

Servings: 04

Ingredients:

Salad:

- 6 ounces vermicelli noodles, boiled
- 2 medium whole carrots, ribboned
- 2 stalks green onions, chopped
- ¼ cup cilantro, chopped
- 2 tablespoons mint, chopped
- 1 cup packed spinach, chopped
- 1 cup red cabbage, sliced
- 1 medium red bell pepper, sliced

Dressing:

- ⅓ cup creamy peanut butter
- 3 tablespoons tamari
- 3 tablespoons maple syrup
- 1 teaspoon chili garlic sauce
- 1 medium lime, juiced
- ¼ cup water

How to Prepare:

1. Combine all the dressing ingredients in a small bowl.

2. In a salad bowl, toss in the noodles, salad, and dressing.

3. Mix them well then refrigerate to chill.

4. Serve.

Nutritional Values:

Calories 361

Total Fat 16.3 g

Saturated Fat 4.9 g

Cholesterol 114 mg

Sodium 515 mg

Total Carbs 29.3 g

Fiber 0.1 g

Sugar 18.2 g

Protein 3.3 g

SOUPS AND STEWS

Sweet Potato Soup

Preparation Time: 20 Minutes

Servings: 2

Ingredients:

- 2 large sweet potatoes, peeled and chopped
- 1 medium carrot, sliced
- 1 medium onion, finely chopped
- 2 cups vegetable broth
- 2 garlic cloves, finely chopped
- 1 tsp salt
- ½ tsp black pepper, freshly ground
- 1 tbsp olive oil

Directions:

1. Plug in your instant pot and press "Sautee" button. Grease the stainless steel insert and add potatoes, onions, and garlic. Stir-fry for 3-4 minutes, or until onions translucent.

2. Now, add the remaining ingredients and stir well until combined. Close the lid and adjust the steam release handle. Press "Manual" button and set the timer for 7 minutes. Cooking Time: on high pressure.

3. When done, press "Cancel" button and perform a quick release. Let it stand for 10 minutes before opening.

4. Enjoy!

5.

Pearl Barley Tomato Mushroom Soup

Preparation Time: 6 Minutes

Servings: 6

Ingredients:

- 1(14-ouncecan crushed tomatoes
- ½cup pearl barley
- ½ounce dried porcini mushrooms, rinsed
- 1ounces cremini mushrooms, sliced
- 2teaspoons olive oil (optional
- 1large carrot, chopped
- 5cups vegetable broth
- 1large yellow onion, chopped
- Salt and freshly ground black pepper
- 1teaspoon dried thyme
- 4ounces shiitake mushrooms, stemmed and sliced
- 2tablespoons soy sauce

Directions:

1. Add the oil in your instant pot.
2. Toss the onion and make it caramelized.
3. Add the remaining ingredients.
4. Mix well and Cooking Time: for 5 minutes with the lid on.
5. Serve warm.
6.

Greek Lentil Soup

Preparation time: 10 minutes

Cooking time: 6 hours 2 minutes

Total time: 6 hours 12 minutes

Servings: 04

Ingredients:

Soup:

- 1 cup lentils
- 1 medium sweet onion, chopped
- 2 large carrots, chopped
- 2 sticks of celery, chopped
- 4 cups veggie broth
- Olive oil to sauté
- 4 tablespoons tomato sauce
- 3 cloves garlic
- 3 bay leaves
- Salt, to taste
- Black pepper, to taste
- Dried oregano, to taste

Toppings:

- Vinegar
- Lemon juice
- Hot sauce

How to Prepare:

1. In a slow cooker, add olive oil and onion.

2. Sauté for 2 minutes then add the rest of the soup ingredients.

3. Put on the slow cooker's lid and Cooking Time: for 6 hours on low heat.

4. Serve warm with the vinegar, lemon juice, and hot sauce.

Nutritional Values:

Calories 231

Total Fat 20.1 g

Saturated Fat 2.4 g

Cholesterol 110 mg

Sodium 941 mg

Total Carbs 20.1 g

Fiber 0.9 g

Sugar 1.4 g

Protein 4.6 g

Zucchini-Dill Bowls With Ricotta Cheese

Preparation Time: 10 minutes

Cooking Time: 25 minutes

Serving Size: 4

Ingredients:

- 4 zucchinis, spiralized and chopped roughly
- Salt and freshly ground black pepper to taste
- ¼ tsp Dijon mustard
- 1 tbsp olive oil
- 1 tbsp freshly squeezed lemon juice
- ½ cup baby spinach
- 1 tbsp freshly chopped tarragon
- 2/3 cup ricotta cheese
- 2 tbsp toasted pine nuts

Directions:

1. Place zucchinis in a medium bowl and season with salt and black pepper.
2. In a small bowl, whisk mustard, olive oil, and lemon juice. Pour mixture over zucchini and toss well.
3. Add spinach, tarragon, ricotta cheese, and pine nuts. Mix with two ladles and serve.

Nutrition:

Calories 857, Total Fat 36.33g, Total Carbs 12.46g, Fiber 2.4g, Net Carbs 10.06g, Protein 26.13g

Corn Chowder

Preparation Time: 5 Minutes

Servings: 4

Ingredients:

- 4cups fresh corn kernels
- 1onion, chopped
- 2chipotle chilies in adobo, minced
- Salt and black pepper
- 1celery rib, chopped
- 4cups vegetable broth
- 1Potato, peeled and diced

Directions:

1. Add the corn kernels, onion, chiles in adobo, seasoning, celery rib, and potato in your instant pot.
2. Pour in the broth and mix well.
3. Cooking Time: for 10 minutes.
4. Use a hand blender to blend the mixture.
5. Serve warm.

Nutritional Values:

Calories 205

Total Fat 22.7 g

Saturated Fat 6.1 g

Cholesterol 4 mg

Sodium 227 mg

Total Carbs 26.1 g

Fiber 1.4 g

Sugar 0.9 g

Protein 5.2 g

Italian Plum Tomato Soup

Preparation Time: 10 Minutes

Servings: 6

Ingredients:

- 1 (28-ouncecan Italian plum tomatoes
- ½ cup nondairy milk
- 1 large yellow onion, chopped
- 1 teaspoon dried marjoram
- 1 (14-ouncecan crushed tomatoes
- 1 cup vegetable broth
- 2 tablespoons tomato paste
- 1 teaspoon dried basil
- 1 teaspoon brown sugar
- ¼ cup oil-packed sun-dried tomatoes, chopped
- 2 garlic cloves, minced
- Salt and freshly ground black pepper

Directions:

1. In an instant pot add the oil with garlic, onion and tomato paste.
2. Cooking Time: for 1 minute and add the marjoram, basil, brown sugar and Cooking Time: for another minute.
3. Add the rest of the ingredients and mix well.
4. Add the lid and Cooking Time: for about 5 minutes.

5. Transfer the mix to a blender.

6. Blend until smooth and serve warm.

Artichoke Bean Soup

Preparation time: 10 minutes

Cooking time: 20 minutes

Total time: 30 minutes

Servings: 04

Ingredients:

- 1 (15 ouncecan artichoke hearts
- ½ bunch kale, chopped
- 2 cups vegetable broth
- 1 tablespoon dried basil
- 1 tablespoon dried oregano
- 1 teaspoon salt
- ½ teaspoon red pepper flakes
- Black pepper, to taste
- 2 (14 ouncecans roasted tomatoes, diced
- 1 (15 ouncecan white beans, drained

How to Prepare:

1. Add all ingredients to a saucepan.
2. Put on the saucepan's lid and Cooking Time: for 20 minutes on a simmer.
3. Serve warm.

Nutritional Values:

Calories 201

Total Fat 8.9 g

Saturated Fat 4.5 g

Cholesterol 57 mg

Sodium 340 mg

Total Carbs 24.7 g

Fiber 1.2 g

Sugar 1.3 g

Protein 15.3 g

Broccoli White Bean Soup

Preparation time: 10 minutes

Cooking time: 4 hrs. 32 minutes

Total time: 4 hrs. 42 minutes

Servings: 04

Ingredients:

- 1 large bunch broccoli
- 3 cloves garlic
- 1 medium white potato
- ¼ cup carrot, chopped
- 2 cups almond milk
- 1½ cups white beans, cooked
- 1 white onion, chopped
- ¾ teaspoon black pepper
- ¼ teaspoon salt
- ½ teaspoon smoky paprika
- ⅓ cup nutritional yeast
- 1 bay leaf
- 1 cup cooked pasta

How to Prepare:

1. In a slow cooker, add olive oil and onion.
2. Sauté for 2 minutes then toss in the rest of the ingredients except pasta and beans.
3. Put on the slow cooker's lid and Cooking Time: for 4

hours on low heat.

4. Once done, add pasta and beans to the soup and mix gently.

5. Cover the soup and remove it from the heat then leave it for another 30 minutes.

6. Serve warm.

Nutritional Values:

Calories 361

Total Fat 16.3 g

Saturated Fat 4.9 g

Cholesterol 114 mg

Sodium 515 mg

Total Carbs 29.3 g

Fiber 0.1 g

Sugar 18.2 g

Protein 3.3 g

Chinese Rice Soup

Preparation time: 10 minutes

Cooking time: 3 hrs.

Total time: 3hrs. 10 minutes

Servings: 04

Ingredients:

Congee:

- 1 cup of white rice (uncooked
- 2-inch piece fresh ginger, minced
- 4 cloves garlic, minced
- 10 cups water
- 14 dried shiitake mushrooms

Toppings:

- Green onions
- Cilantro
- Sesame seeds
- Hot sauce
- Toasted sesame oil
- Soy sauce
- Peanuts
- Chili oil
- Shelled edamame

How to Prepare:

1. Add all the ingredients to a slow cooker.

2. Put on the slow cooker's lid and Cooking Time: for 3 hours on low heat.

3. Once done, garnish with desired toppings.

4. Serve warm.

Nutritional Values:

Calories 210.6

Total Fat 10.91g

Saturated Fat 7.4g

Sodium 875 mg

Potassium 604 mg

Carbohydrates 25.6g

Fiber 4.3g

Sugar 7.9g

Protein 2.1g

Balsamic Hatchet Soup

Preparation Time: 20 Minutes

Servings: 4

A hatchet soup is one where you combine any number of different ingredients, and is great for using up a medley of vegetables.

Ingredients:

- 3 shallots, halved
- 3 garlic cloves, minced
- 6 ounces green beans, trimmed and halved
- 1 red or yellow bell pepper, seeded and cut into ¼-inch strips
- 8 ounces mushrooms, halved, quartered, or sliced
- 3 small zucchini, halved lengthwise and cut into ¼-inch slices
- 2 small yellow summer squash, halved lengthwise and cut into ¼-inch slices
- 1½ cups cherry tomatoes, halved
- ½ cup balsamic reduction
- 3 tablespoons chopped fresh basil
- 2 tablespoons chopped fresh flat-leaf parsley
- 2 teaspoons olive oil
- Salt and freshly ground black pepper

Directions:

1. Put the oil in your instant pot and warm.
2. Add the shallots and soften for 3 minutes.
3. Add the garlic and Cooking Time: another minute.
4. Add the green beans, bell pepper, mushrooms, zucchini, and yellow squash.
5. Seal and Cooking Time: on Stew for 10 minutes.
6. Depressurize quickly, add the tomato, basil, and parsley.
7. Reseal and Cooking Time: on Stew 2 minutes.
8. Depressurize naturally and serve drizzled with balsamic reduction.

Cauliflower Soup

Preparation time: 10 minutes

Cooking time: 4 hours 5 minutes

Total time: 4 hours 15 minutes

Servings: 04

Ingredients:

- 2 tablespoons olive oil
- 1½ cups sweet white onion, chopped
- 2 large cloves of garlic, chopped
- 1 head cauliflower, cut into florets
- 1 cup coconut milk
- 1 cup filtered water
- 1 teaspoon vegetable stock paste
- 2 tablespoons nutritional yeast
- Dash of olive oil
- Fresh cracked pepper
- Parsley, to serve

How to prepare:

1. Add olive oil and onion to a slow cooker.
2. Sauté for 5 minutes then add the rest of the ingredients.
3. Put on the slow cooker's lid and Cooking Time: for 4 hours on low heat.
4. Once done, blend the soup with a hand blender.
5. Garnish with parsley, and cracked pepper

6. Serve.

Nutritional Values:

Calories 119

Total Fat 14 g

Saturated Fat 2 g

Cholesterol 65 mg

Sodium 269 mg

Total Carbs 19 g

Fiber 4 g

Sugar 6 g

Protein 5g

African Lentil Soup

Preparation time: 10 minutes

Cooking time: 20 minutes

Total time: 30 minutes

Servings: 4

Ingredients:

- 1 teaspoon oil
- ½ medium onion, chopped
- 2 juicy tomatoes, chopped
- 4 garlic cloves, chopped
- 1-inch piece of ginger, chopped
- 1 tablespoon Sambal Oelek
- 1 tablespoon tomato paste
- 1½ teaspoons ground cumin
- 2 teaspoons ground coriander
- 1 teaspoon Harissa Spice Blend
- ¼ teaspoon black pepper
- ¼ cup nut butter
- 2 tablespoons peanuts
- ½ cup red lentils
- 2½ cups vegetable stock
- ¾ teaspoon salt
- 1 teaspoon lemon juice
- ½ cup packed baby spinach

How to Prepare:

1. In a slow cooker, add olive oil and onion.
2. Sauté for 5 minutes then toss in rest of the ingredients except peanuts.
3. Put on the slow cooker's lid and Cooking Time: for 5 hours on low heat.
4. Once done, garnish with peanuts.
5. Serve.

SNACK

Beetroot Hummus

Preparation Time: 10 minutes

Cooking Time: 60 minutes

Servings: 4

Ingredients:

- 15 ounces cooked chickpeas
- 3 small beets
- 1 teaspoon minced garlic
- 1/2 teaspoon smoked paprika
- 1 teaspoon of sea salt
- 1/4 teaspoon red chili flakes
- 2 tablespoons olive oil
- 1 lemon, juiced
- 2 tablespoon tahini
- 1 tablespoon chopped almonds
- 1 tablespoon chopped cilantro

Directions:

1. Drizzle oil over beets, season with salt, then wrap beets in a foil and bake for 60 minutes at 425 degrees F until tender.

2. When done, let beet cool for 10 minutes, then peel and dice them and place them in a food processor.

3. Add remaining ingredients and pulse for 2 minutes until smooth, tip the hummus in a bowl, drizzle with some more oil, and then serve straight away.

Nutrition:

Calories: 50.1 Cal

Fat: 2.5 g

Carbs: 5 g

Protein: 2 g

Fiber: 1 g

Seasoned Potatoes

Preparation time: 10 minutes

Cooking time: 12 minutes

Total time: 22 minutes

Servings: 04

Ingredients:

- 1 tablespoon coriander seeds
- ½ teaspoon turmeric powder
- ½ teaspoon red chili powder
- 1 teaspoon pomegranate powder
- 1 tablespoon pickled mango, chopped
- 1 tablespoon cumin seeds
- 2 teaspoons fenugreeks, dried
- 5 potatoes, boiled, peeled and cubed
- Salt and black pepper to the taste
- 2 tablespoons olive oil

How to Prepare:

1. Take a baking dish suitable to fit in your air fryer.
2. Add oil, coriander, and cumin seeds to the dish.
3. Place it over medium heat and sauté for 2 minutes.
4. Stir in the rest of the ingredients.
5. Mix well then spread the potatoes in the air fryer basket.
6. Seal it and Cooking Time: them for 10 minutes at 360

degrees F on Air fryer mode.

7. Serve warm.

Nutritional Values:

Calories 201

Total Fat 8.9 g

Saturated Fat 4.5 g

Cholesterol 57 mg

Sodium 340 mg

Total Carbs 24.7 g

Fiber 1.2 g

Sugar 1.3 g

Protein 15.3 g

Spinach Stuffed Portobello

Preparation time: 10 minutes

Cooking time: 12 minutes

Total time: 22 minutes

Servings: 4

Ingredients:

- 4 portobello mushrooms, chopped
- 10 basil leaves
- 1 tablespoon parsley
- ¼ cup olive oil
- 8 cherry tomatoes, halved
- 1 cup baby spinach
- 3 garlic cloves, chopped
- 1 cup almonds, chopped
- Salt and black pepper to the taste

Mushroom Stuffed Tomatoes

Preparation time: 10 minutes

Cooking time: 15 minutes

Total time: 25 minutes

Servings: 04

Ingredients:

- 4 tomatoes, tops removed and pulp removed (reserve for filling
- 1 yellow onion, chopped
- ½ cup mushrooms, chopped
- 1 tablespoon bread crumbs
- 1 tablespoon vegan butter
- ¼ teaspoon caraway seeds
- 1 tablespoon parsley, chopped
- 2 tablespoons celery, chopped
- 1 cup vegan cheese, shredded
- Salt and black pepper to the taste

How to Prepare:

1. Place a pan over medium heat, add butter.
2. When it melts, add onion and celery to sauté for 3 minutes.
3. Stir in mushrooms and tomato pulp.
4. Cooking Time: for 1 minute then add crumbled bread, pepper, salt, cheese, parsley, and caraway seeds.

5. Cooking Time: while stirring for 4 minutes then remove from the heat.

6. After cooling the mixture, stuff it equally in the tomatoes.

7. Place the tomatoes in the air fryer basket and seal it.

8. Cooking Time: them for 8 minutes at 350 degrees F on air fryer mode.

9. Enjoy.

Nutritional Values:

Calories 361

Total Fat 16.3 g

Saturated Fat 4.9 g

Cholesterol 114 mg

Sodium 515 mg

Total Carbs 29.3 g

Fiber 0.1 g

Sugar 18.2 g

Protein 3.3 g

How to Prepare:

1. Add all ingredients except mushrooms to a food processor.
2. Blend it all well until smooth then stuff each mushroom cap with the mixture.
3. Place the stuffed mushrooms in the air fryer basket and seal it.
4. Cooking Time: them for 12 minutes at 350 degrees F on air fryer mode.
5. Enjoy.

Nutritional Values:

Calories 205

Total Fat 22.7 g

Saturated Fat 6.1 g

Cholesterol 4 mg

Sodium 227 mg

Total Carbs 26.1 g

Fiber 1.4 g

Sugar 0.9 g

Protein 5.2 g

Black Bean Lime Dip

Preparation Time: 5 minutes

Cooking Time: 6 minutes

Servings: 4

Ingredients:

- 15.5 ounces cooked black beans
- 1 teaspoon minced garlic
- ½ of a lime, juiced
- 1 inch of ginger, grated
- 1/3 teaspoon salt
- 1/3 teaspoon ground black pepper
- 1 tablespoon olive oil

Directions:

1. Take a frying pan, add oil and when hot, add garlic and ginger and Cooking Time: for 1 minute until fragrant.
2. Then add beans, splash with some water and fry for 3 minutes until hot.
3. Season beans with salt and black pepper, drizzle with lime juice, then remove the pan from heat and mash the beans until smooth pasta comes together.
4. Serve the dip with whole-grain breadsticks or vegetables.

Nutrition:

Calories: 374 Cal

Fat: 14 g

Carbs: 46 g

Protein: 15 g

Fiber: 17 g

SAUCES, AND CONDIMENTS

Hot Sauce

Preparation time: 10 minutes

Cooking time: 15 minutes

Servings: 6

Ingredients:

- 4 Serrano peppers, destemmed
- 1/2 of medium white onion, chopped
- 1 medium carrot, chopped
- 10 habanero chilies, destemmed
- 6 cloves of garlic, unpeeled
- 2 teaspoons sea salt
- 1 cup apple cider vinegar
- 1/2 teaspoon brown rice syrup
- 1 cup of water

Directions:

1. Take a skillet pan, place it medium heat, add garlic, and Cooking Time: for 15 minutes until roasted, frequently turning garlic, set aside to cool.

2. Meanwhile, take a saucepan, place it over medium-low heat, add remaining ingredients in it, except for salt and syrup, stir and Cooking Time: for 12 minutes until vegetables are tender.

3. When the garlic has roasted and cooled, peel them and add them to a food processor.

4. Then add cooked saucepan along with remaining ingredients, and pulse for 3 minutes until smooth.

5. Let sauce cool and then serve straight away

Nutrition Value:

Calories: 137 Cal

Fat: 0 g

Carbs: 30 g

Protein: 4 g

Fiber: 10 g

Spicy Red Wine Tomato Sauce

Preparation time: 5 minutes

Cooking time: 1 hour

Servings: 4

Ingredients:

- 28 ounces puree of whole tomatoes, peeled
- 4 cloves of garlic, peeled
- 1 tablespoon dried basil
- ¼ teaspoon ground black pepper
- 1 tablespoon dried oregano
- ¼ teaspoon red pepper flakes
- 1 tablespoon dried sage
- 1 tablespoon dried thyme
- 3 teaspoon coconut sugar
- 1/2 of lemon, juice
- 1/4 cup red wine

Directions:

1. Take a large saucepan, place it over medium heat, add tomatoes and remaining ingredients, stir and simmer for 1 hour or more until thickened and cooked.
2. Serve sauce over pasta.

Nutrition Value:

Calories: 110 Cal

Fat: 2.5 g

Carbs: 9 g

Protein: 2 g

Fiber: 2 g

Hot Sauce

Preparation time: 5 minutes

Cooking time: 0 minute

Servings: 16

Ingredients:

- 4 cloves of garlic, peeled
- 15 Hot peppers, de-stemmed, chopped
- 1/2 teaspoon. coriander
- 1/2 teaspoon. sea salt
- 1/2 teaspoon. red chili powder
- 1/2 of lime, zested
- 1/4 teaspoon. cumin
- 1/2 lime, juiced
- 1 cup apple cider vinegar

Directions:

1. Place all the ingredients in the order in a food processor or blender and then pulse for 3 to 5 minutes at high speed until smooth.
2. Tip the sauce in a bowl and then serve.

Nutrition Value:

Calories: 5 Cal

Fat: 0 g

Carbs: 1 g

Protein: 0 g

Fiber: 0.3 g

Vodka Cream Sauce

Preparation time: 5 minutes

Cooking time: 5 minutes

Servings: 1

Ingredients:

- 1/4 cup cashews, unsalted , soaked in warm water for 15 minutes
- 24-ounce marinara sauce
- 2 tablespoons vodka
- 1/4 cup water

Directions:

1. Drain the cashews, transfer them in a food processor, pour in water, and blend for 2 minutes until smooth.
2. Tip the mixture in a pot, stir in pasta sauce and vodka and simmer for 3 minutes over medium heat until done, stirring constantly.
3. Serve sauce over pasta.

Nutrition Value:

Calories: 207 Cal

Fat: 16 g

Carbs: 9.2 g

Protein: 2.4 g

Fiber: 4.3 g

DESSERTS AND DRINKS

Lemon Squares

Preparation time: 10 minutes

Cooking time: 30 minutes

Servings: 6

Ingredients:

- 1 cup whole wheat flour
- ½ cup vegetable oil
- 1 and ¼ cups coconut sugar
- 1 medium banana
- 2 teaspoons lemon peel, grated
- 2 tablespoons lemon juice
- 2 tablespoons flax meal combined with 2 tablespoons water
- ½ teaspoon baking powder

Directions:

1. In a bowl, mix flour with ¼ cup sugar and oil, stir well, press on the bottom of a pan that fits your air fryer, introduce in the fryer and bake at 350 degrees F for 14 minutes.
2. In another bowl, mix the rest of the sugar with lemon juice, lemon peel, banana, and baking powder, stir using your mixer and spread over baked crust.
3. Bake for 15 minutes more, leave aside to cool down, cut into medium squares and serve cold.
4. Enjoy!

Nutrition: calories 140, fat 4, fiber 1, carbs 12, protein 1

Green Popsicle

Preparation time: 10 minutes

Cooking time: 2 hours

Total time: 2 hours and 10 minutes

Servings: 4

Ingredients:

- 1 ripe avocado, peeled and pitted
- 1 cup fresh spinach
- 1 can (13.5 ouncefull fat coconut milk
- ¼ cup lime juice
- 2 tablespoons maple syrup
- 1 teaspoon vanilla extract

How to Prepare:

1. In a blender, blend all the ingredients for popsicles until smooth.
2. Divide the popsicle blend into the popsicle molds.
3. Insert the popsicles sticks and close the molds.
4. Place the molds in the freezer for 2 hours to set.
5. Serve.

Nutritional Values:

Calories 361

Total Fat 16.3 g

Saturated Fat 4.9 g

Cholesterol 114 mg

Sodium 515 mg

Total Carbs 29.3 g

Fiber 0.1 g

Sugar 18.2 g

Protein 3.3 g

Tangerine Cake

Preparation time: 10 minutes

Cooking time: 20 minutes

Servings: 8

Ingredients:

- ¾ cup coconut sugar
- 2 cups whole wheat flour
- ¼ cup olive oil
- ½ cup almond milk
- 1 teaspoon cider vinegar
- ½ teaspoon vanilla extract
- Juice and zest of 2 lemons
- Juice and zest of 1 tangerine

Directions:

1. In a bowl, mix flour with sugar and stir.
2. In another bowl, mix oil with milk, vinegar, vanilla extract, lemon juice and zest, tangerine zest and flour, whisk very well, pour this into a cake pan that fits your air fryer, introduce in the fryer and Cooking Time: at 360 degrees F for 20 minutes.
3. Serve right away.
4. Enjoy!

Nutrition: calories 210, fat 1, fiber 1, carbs 6, protein 4

Fudge Popsicles

Preparation time: 10 minutes

Cooking time: 2 hours

Total time: 2 hours and 10 minutes

Servings: 2

Ingredients:

- 1 cup almond milk
- 3 ripe bananas
- 3 tablespoon cocoa powder
- 1 tablespoon almond butter

How to Prepare:

1. In a blender, blend all the ingredients for popsicles until smooth.
2. Divide the popsicle blend into the popsicle molds.
3. Insert the popsicles sticks and close the molds.
4. Place the molds in the freezer for 2 hours to set.
5. Serve.

Nutritional Values:

Calories 201

Total Fat 8.9 g

Saturated Fat 4.5 g

Cholesterol 57 mg

Sodium 340 mg

Total Carbs 24.7 g

Fiber 1.2 g

Sugar 1.3 g

Protein 15.3 g

Grape Pudding

Preparation time: 10 minutes

Cooking time: 40 minutes

Servings: 6

Ingredients:

- 1 cup grapes curd
- 3 cups grapes
- 3 and ½ ounces maple syrup
- 3 tablespoons flax meal combined with 3 tablespoons water
- 2 ounces coconut butter, melted
- 3 and ½ ounces almond milk
- ½ cup almond flour
- ½ teaspoon baking powder

Directions:

1. In a bowl, mix the half of the fruit curd with the grapes stir and divide into 6 heatproof ramekins.
2. In a bowl, mix flax meal with maple syrup, melted coconut butter, the rest of the curd, baking powder, milk and flour and stir well.
3. Divide this into the ramekins as well, introduce in the fryer and Cooking Time: at 200 degrees F for 40 minutes.

4. Leave puddings to cool down and serve!

5. Enjoy!

Nutrition: calories 230, fat 22, fiber 3, carbs 17, protein 8

Strawberry Coconut Popsicles

Preparation time: 10 minutes

Cooking time: 2 hours

Total time: 2 hours and 10 minutes

Servings: 2

Ingredients:

- 2 medium bananas, sliced
- 1 can coconut milk
- 1 cup strawberries
- 3 tablespoons maple syrup

How to Prepare:

1. In a blender, blend all the ingredients for popsicles until smooth.
2. Divide the popsicle blend into the popsicle molds.
3. Insert the popsicles sticks and close the molds.
4. Place the molds in the freezer for 2 hours to set.
5. Serve.

Nutritional Values:

Calories 205

Total Fat 22.7 g

Saturated Fat 6.1 g

Cholesterol 4 mg

Sodium 227 mg

Total Carbs 26.1 g

Fiber 1.4 g

Sugar 0.9 g

Protein 5.2 g

Sweet Cashew Sticks

Preparation time: 10 minutes

Cooking time: 15 minutes

Servings: 6

Ingredients:

- 1/3 cup stevia
- ¼ cup almond meal
- 1 tablespoon almond butter
- 1 and ½ cups cashews, chopped
- 4 dates, chopped
- ¾ cup coconut, shredded
- 1 tablespoon chia seeds

Directions:

1. In a bowl, mix stevia with almond meal, almond butter, cashews, coconut, dates and chia seeds and stir well again.
2. Spread this on a lined baking sheet that fits your air fryer, press well, introduce in the fryer and Cooking Time: at 300 degrees F for 15 minutes.
3. Leave mix to cool down, cut into medium sticks and serve.
4. Enjoy!

Nutrition: calories 162, fat 4, fiber 7, carbs 5, protein 6

Sweet Tomato Bread

Preparation time: 10 minutes

Cooking time: 30 minutes

Servings: 4

Ingredients:

- 1 and ½ cups whole wheat flour
- 1 teaspoon cinnamon powder
- 1 teaspoon baking powder
- 1 teaspoon baking soda
- ¾ cup maple syrup
- 1 cup tomatoes, chopped
- ½ cup olive oil
- 2 tablespoon apple cider vinegar

Directions:

1. In a bowl, mix flour with baking powder, baking soda, cinnamon and maple syrup and stir well.
2. In another bowl, mix tomatoes with olive oil and vinegar and stir well.
3. Combine the 2 mixtures, stir well, pour into a greased loaf pan that fits your air fryer, introduce in the fryer and Cooking Time: at 360 degrees F for 30 minutes.
4. Leave the cake to cool down, slice and serve.
5. Enjoy!

Nutrition: calories 203, fat 2, fiber 1, carbs 12, protein 4